T O

_____

F R O M

_____

**Traveling Light**

Published by Blessings Unlimited®, a brand of DaySpring Cards®, Inc.
Siloam Springs, Arkansas

Design by Garborg Design Works

ISBN 1-58061-500-7

Haven't you been known to pick up a few bags? Odds are, you did this morning. Somewhere between the first step on the floor and the last step out the door, you grabbed some luggage. You stepped over to the baggage carousel and loaded up. Don't remember doing so? That's because you did it without thinking.

# JANUARY 1

May the Lord bless you and keep you; the Lord make His face shine upon you and be gracious to you; the Lord turn His face toward you and give you peace.

Numbers 6:24-26 NIV

# DECEMBER 31

Don't remember seeing a baggage terminal? That's because the carousel is not the one in the airport; it's the one in the mind. And the bags we grab are not made of leather; they're made of burdens.

JANUARY 2

As you meet your Shepherd, let him renew and refresh your spirit. I pray that you've left some of your burdens at the foot of the cross. And remember: Regardless of the challenges of life, there is One who cares and will never leave you. "We are his people, the sheep he tends" (Psalm 100:3).

## DECEMBER 30

The suitcase of guilt. A sack of discontent. You drape a duffel bag of weariness on one shoulder and a hanging bag of grief on the other. Add on a backpack of doubt, an overnight bag of loneliness, and a trunk of fear. Pretty soon you're pulling more stuff than a skycap. No wonder you're so tired at the end of the day. Lugging luggage is exhausting.

JANUARY 3

Tomorrow, when out of habit you pick your luggage back up, set it down again. Set it down again and again until that sweet day when you find you aren't picking it back up.

DECEMBER 29

Why is everyone hungry for more?... I have God's more-than-enough, more joy in one ordinary day.... At day's end I'm ready for sound sleep, for you, God, have put my life back together.

PSALM 4:6-8 THE MESSAGE

# JANUARY 4

Let's get rid of the bags! Once and for all, let's give our luggage to him. Let's take him at his word!

*Come to me, all of you who are weary and carry heavy burdens, and I will give you rest.*

MATTHEW 11:28 NLT

# DECEMBER 28

What about your soul? When your heart is hungry, when your dreams are thirsty, when your spirit has run dry. Where do you turn? I'd like to urge you to turn to your Shepherd. Jesus invites, "Come to me, all of you who are weary and carry heavy burdens, and I will give you rest" (Matthew 11:28 NLT).

# JANUARY 5

Do we not dwell in the gallery of our God? Isn't the sky his canvas and humanity his magnum opus? Are we not encircled by artistry? Sunsets burning. Waves billowing. And isn't the soul his studio? The birthing of love, the bequeathing of grace. All around us miracles pop like fireflies—souls are touched, hearts are changed.

DECEMBER 27

If you let him, your Shepherd will refresh your spirit by lightening your load—by releasing you from the burdens you were never intended to bear: burdens of worry, guilt, hopelessness, fear, shame, doubt, loneliness...the burdens of life.

# JANUARY 6

God can do anything, you know—far more than you could ever imagine or guess or request in your wildest dreams!

EPHESIANS 3:20 THE MESSAGE

DECEMBER 26

Take time to eat, drink, and be anointed by your Father. Spend a few moments every day letting him do what he wants to do: take care of you. He knows how; he is your Shepherd.

When you see God, you'll set down your last piece of luggage. You'll drop your longing when you see your Father. Those you love will shout. Those you know will applaud. But all the noise will cease when he cups your chin and says, "Welcome home." And with scarred hands he'll wipe every tear from your eye. And you will dwell in the house of your Lord—forever.

DECEMBER 25

God is saying to you, "Set that stuff down! You're carrying burdens you don't need to bear. Come to me," he invites, "all of you who are weary and carry heavy burdens, and I will give you rest" (Matthew 11:28 NLT).

JANUARY 8

By the moment we enter the door to God's house only one bag will remain. Not guilt. It was dropped at Calvary. Not the fear of death. It was left at the grave. The only lingering luggage will be this God-given longing for home.

DECEMBER 24

If we let him, God will lighten our loads.

JANUARY 9

This is not our forever house. It will serve for the time being. But there is nothing like the moment we enter his door.

DECEMBER 23

I'm asking God for one thing, only one thing: To live with him in his house my whole life long. I'll contemplate his beauty; I'll study at his feet. That's the only quiet, secure place in a noisy world.

PSALM 27:4-5 THE MESSAGE

# JANUARY 10

And, according to God, this is a part of the plan: Every wrinkle and every needle take us one step closer to the last step when Jesus will change our simple bodies into forever bodies. No pain. No depression. No sickness. No end.

# DECEMBER 22

Do more beloved words than the Twenty-third Psalm exist? Framed and hung in hospital halls, scratched on prison walls, quoted by the young, and whispered by the dying. In these lines sailors have found a harbor, the frightened have found a father, and strugglers have found a friend.

## JANUARY 11

Aging is God's idea. It's one of the ways he keeps us headed homeward. We can't change the process, but we can change our attitude. Here is a thought. "We are waiting for God to finish making us his own children, which means our bodies will be made free" (Romans 8:23).

# DECEMBER 21

No one has to remind you of the high cost of anxiety. Worry divides the mind. The biblical word for worry (merimnao) is a compound of two Greek words, merizo (to divide) and nous (the mind). Anxiety splits our energy between today's priorities and tomorrow's problems. Father, give me the courage to place in your hands all of my worries. And give me the faith to leave them with you.

JANUARY 12

Not one is missing, not one forgotten. God the Father has his eye on each of you.... May everything good from God be yours!

1 PETER 1:1-2 THE MESSAGE

# DECEMBER 20

Do you have some luggage of your own? Do you think God might use the Twenty-third Psalm to lighten your load? Traveling light means trusting God with the burdens you were never intended to bear.

JANUARY 13

Aging. It's no fun. The way we try to avoid it, you'd think we could. We paint the body, preserve the body, protect the body. And well we should. These bodies are God's gifts. We should be responsible. But we should also be realistic. This body must die so the new body can live. "Flesh and blood cannot have a part in the kingdom of God. Some-thing that will ruin cannot have a part in something that never ruins" (1 Corinthains 15:50).

DECEMBER 19

Why don't you try traveling light? Have you ever considered the impact that excess baggage has on relationships? How do you embrace someone if your arms are full of bags? For the sake of those you love, learn to set them down.

# JANUARY 14

Homesickness is one of the burdens God doesn't mind if we carry. God has "set eternity in the hearts of men" (Ecclesiastes 3:11 NIV). Down deep you know you are not home yet.

DECEMBER 18

For the sake of the God you serve, learn to travel light. He wants to use you, you know. But how can he if you are exhausted?

# JANUARY 15

The twists and turns of life have a way of reminding us—we aren't home here. This is not our homeland. We aren't fluent in the languages of disease and death. The culture confuses the heart, the noise disrupts our sleep, and we feel far from home. And, you know what? That's OK.

DECEMBER 17

Through the heartfelt mercies of our God,
God's Sunrise will break in upon us...
showing us the way, one foot at a time,
down the path of peace.

LUKE 1:78-79 THE MESSAGE

# JANUARY 16

Where will you live forever? In the house of the Lord. If his house is your "forever house," what does that make this earthly house? You got it! Short-term housing. This is not our home. "Our homeland is in heaven" (Philippians 3:20).

DECEMBER 16

God has a great race for you to run. Under his care you will go where you've never been and serve in ways you've never dreamed. But you have to drop some stuff. How can you share grace if you are full of guilt?

JANUARY 17

You're being prepared for your Master's house. "And I will dwell in the house of the Lord forever" (Psalm 23:6 NKJV).

DECEMBER 15

For the sake of those you love, travel light.
For the sake of the God you serve, travel light.

JANUARY 18

Rest from doubt. Why? Because God follows you.

DECEMBER 14

God has a great race for you to run. Under his care you will go where you've never been and serve in ways you've never dreamed. But you have to drop some stuff. How can you offer comfort if you are disheartened?

JANUARY 19

God can pour on the blessings in astonishing ways so that you're ready for anything and everything, more than just ready to do what needs to be done.... This most generous God who gives seed to the farmer that becomes bread for your meals is more than extravagant with you.

2 CORINTHIANS 9:8,10 THE MESSAGE

DECEMBER 13

For the sake of your own joy, travel light. There are certain weights in life you simply cannot carry. Your Lord is asking you to set them down and trust him. He is the father at the baggage claim.

JANUARY 20

Using all of his power, God convinces us that he is who he is and that he can be trusted to lead us home. His goodness and mercy will follow us all the days of our lives.

# DECEMBER 12

God has a great race for you to run. Under his care you will go where you've never been and serve in ways you've never dreamed. But you have to drop some stuff. How can you lift someone else's load if your arms are full with your own?

JANUARY 21

Most of all, God gives us himself. Even when we choose our hovel over his house and our trash over his grace, still he follows. Never forcing us. Never leaving us. Patiently persistent. Faithfully present.

DECEMBER 11

**W**hoever serves me must follow me; and where I am, my servant also will be. My Father will honor the one who serves me.

JOHN 12:26 NIV

# JANUARY 22

We have doubted our Helper, but God has followed us. We are quick to turn away, but God is slow to anger and detemined to stay. We don't accept God's gifts, but God still gives them. He gives us his angels, placed on our path.

# December 10

When a dad sees his five-year-old son trying to drag the family trunk off the carousel, what does he say? The father will say to his son what God is saying to you. "Set it down, child. I'll carry that one."

See the big picture, not the small. Perhaps your home and health have been threatened. The immediate result might be pain. But the long-term result might be finding a Father you never knew. A Father who will follow you all the days of your life.

DECEMBER 9

What do you say we take God up on his offer? We just might find ourselves traveling a little lighter. I can't overstate God's promise: "Unload all your worries onto him, since he is looking after you" (1 Peter 5:7 JB).

# JANUARY 24

God follows you. Why? Because you are family, and he will follow you all the days of your life.

## DECEMBER 8

God leads us. He tells us what we need to know when we need to know it. Lord, thank you for being my Shepherd. Today I'll entrust my worries to you because I know that you will lead me.

# JANUARY 25

Take your everyday, ordinary life—your sleeping, eating, going-to-work, and walking-around life—and place it before God as an offering. Embracing what God does for you is the best thing you can do for him.

ROMANS 12:1 THE MESSAGE

# DECEMBER 7

Honestly, now. Did God save you so you would fret? Would he teach you to walk just to watch you fall? Would he be nailed to the cross for your sins and then disregard your prayers? Come on. Is Scripture teasing us when it reads, "He has put his angels in charge of you to watch over you wherever you go" (Psalm 91:11)?
I don't think so either.

## JANUARY 26

Measure your value through God's eyes, not your own. There are times in our lives when we are gangrels—homeless, disoriented, hard to help, and hard to love. In those seasons remember this simple fact: God loves you.

# December 6

He places himself between you and the need. And at the right time, he gives you the ticket. This is the same promise God gave the children of Israel. He promised to supply them with manna each day. But he told them to collect only one day's supply at a time. Those who disobeyed and collected enough for two days found themselves with rotten manna. God gave them what they needed, in their time of need.

JANUARY 27

Trust your faith and not your feelings. You don't feel spiritual each day? Of course you don't. But your feelings have no impact on God's presence. On the days you don't feel close to God, trust your faith and not your feelings. Goodness and mercy shall follow you all the days of your life.

# DECEMBER 5

God will do the right thing at the right time. What a difference that makes. Father, thank you for being ever present in my life.

JANUARY 28

I wonder...have you sensed God's presence? If so, then release your doubts. Set them down. Be encumbered by them no longer. You are no candidate for insecurity. You are no longer a client of timidity. You can trust God. He has given his love to you; why don't you give your doubts to him?

DECEMBER 4

Father, forgive me for worrying. Thank you for reminding me how much you care for me and my problems.

# JANUARY 29

God is the God who follows. I wonder...have you sensed him following you? Through the kindness of a stranger. The majesty of a sunset. The mystery of romance. Through the question of a child or the commitment of a spouse. Through a word well spoken or a touch well timed, have you sensed his presence?

DECEMBER 3

Ask and you'll get; Seek and you'll find; Knock and the door will open. Don't bargain with God. Be direct. Ask for what you need.

LUKE 11:9-10 THE MESSAGE

# JANUARY 30

I look behind me and you're there, then up ahead and you're there, too—your reassuring presence, coming and going. This is too much, too wonderful—I can't take it all in!

PSALM 139:5-6 THE MESSAGE

# DECEMBER 2

Lord, I need your holy strength today. Please give me what you think is best to help me face the struggles of this day.

JANUARY 31

Peter had denied his Lord and gone back to fishing when he heard his name and looked over his shoulder and saw Jesus cooking breakfast. God had followed him in spite of his failure.

# DECEMBER 1

Father, your grace truly is sufficient for me. Thank you, Gracious Lord, for watching over me and calming my anxious heart.

*The Lord is good, a refuge in times of trouble. He cares for those who trust in him.*

NAHUM 1:7 NIV

# FEBRUARY 1

Lazarus was three days dead in a sealed tomb when he heard a voice, lifted his head, and looked over his shoulder and saw Jesus standing. God had followed him into death.

# November 30

Rest from the shadow of grief.
Why? Because God guides you.

# FEBRUARY 2

John the Apostle was banished on Patmos when he looked over his shoulder and saw the skies begin to open. God had followed him into his exile.

NOVEMBER 29

"The Lord" (Psalm 23:1). David is concerned that you and I don't make the mistake of worshiping a man-made god. His pen has scarcely touched papyrus, and he's urging us to avoid gods of our own making. With his very first words in this psalm, David sets out to deliver us from the burden of a lesser deity.

FEBRUARY 3

An unnamed Samaritan woman knew God's pursuing love. She was alone in life and alone at the well when she looked over her shoulder and heard a Messiah speaking. God had followed her through her pain.

NOVEMBER 28

Though David will speak of green pastures, his thesis is not rest. He will describe death's somber valley, but this poem is not an ode to dying. He will tell of the Lord's forever house, but his theme is not heaven. Why did David write the Twenty-third Psalm? To build our trust in God...to remind us of who he is.

The disciples of Jesus knew the feeling of being followed by God. They were rain soaked and shivering when they looked over their shoulders and saw Jesus walking toward them. God had followed them into the storm.

NOVEMBER 27

In the Twenty-third Psalm David devotes one hundred and fifteen words to explaining the first two: "The Lord." In the arena of unnecessary luggage, the psalmist begins with the weightiest: the refashioned god. One who looks nice but does little.

FEBRUARY 5

Jonah can tell you about how God sought him. He was a fugitive on a boat when he looked over his shoulder and saw clouds brewing. God had followed him onto the ocean.

NOVEMBER 26

A man-made god may be a genie in a bottle. Convenient. Congenial. Need a parking place, date, field goal made or missed? All you do is rub the bottle and poof—it's yours. And, what's even better, this god goes back into the bottle after he's done. Is that the kind of god you have?

FEBRUARY 6

Moses can tell you about God's loving pursuit. He was forty years in the desert when he looked over his shoulder and saw a bush blazing. God had followed him into the wilderness.

NOVEMBER 25

A man-made god may be a sweet grandpa. So soft hearted. So wise. So kind. But very, very, very old. Grandpas are great when they are awake, but they tend to doze off when you need them. Is that the kind of god you have?

Isn't this the kind of God described in the Bible? A God who follows us? There are many in the Scriptures who would say so. You have to go no farther than the third chapter of the first book before you find God in the role of a seeker. Adam and Eve are hiding in the bushes, partly to cover their bodies, partly to cover their sin. But does God wait for them to come to him? No, the words ring in the garden: "Where are you?" (Genesis 3:9). With that question God began a quest for the heart of humanity that continues up to and through the moment you read these words.

# November 24

A man-made god may be a busy dad. Leaves on Mondays, returns on Saturdays. Lots of road trips and business meetings. He'll show up on Sunday, however, so clean up and look spiritual. On Monday, be yourself again. He'll never know. Is that the kind of god you have?

FEBRUARY 8

David envisions a mobile and active God. Dare we do the same? Dare we envision a God who follows us? Who pursues us? Who chases us? Who tracks us down and wins us over? Who follows us with "goodness and mercy" all the days of our lives?

NOVEMBER 23

If you've viewed God as a genie, a sweet grandpa, or a busy dad, you know the problems that can cause. A busy dad doesn't have time for your questions. A kind grandpa is too weak to carry your load. And if your god is a genie in a bottle, then you are greater than he is. He comes and goes at your command. A god who looks nice but does little. Is that the kind of god you have?

FEBRUARY 9

And what will God do during the days that lie ahead? (Here is my favorite word.) He will "follow" you. What a surprising way to describe God!

NOVEMBER 22

Though foreign to us, the name Yahweh was rich to David. So rich, in fact, that David chose it over El Shaddai (God Almighty), El Elyon (God Most High), and El Olam (God the Everlasting). These and many other titles for God were at David's disposal. But when he considered all the options, David chose Yahweh. Why Yahweh? Because Yahweh is God's name.

FEBRUARY 10

"All the days of my life." Think of the days that lie ahead. What do you see? Days at home with only toddlers? God will be at your side. Days in a dead-end job? He will walk you through. Days of loneliness? He will take your hand. Surely goodness and mercy shall follow me—not some, not most, not nearly all—but all the days of my life.

NOVEMBER 21

I might call you dad, mom, doctor, or student, and those terms may describe you, but they aren't your name. If you want to call me by my name, say Max. If I call you by your name, I say it. And if you want to call God by his name, say Yahweh. God has told us his name. (How he must long to be close to us.)

FEBRUARY 11

"All the days of my life." What a huge statement. Look at the size of it! Goodness and mercy follow the child of God each and every day!

NOVEMBER 20

The name I AM sounds strikingly close to the Hebrew verb to be–havah. It's quite possibly a combination of the present tense form (I am) and the causative tense (I cause to be). Yahweh, then, seems to mean "I am" and "I cause." Why is that important? Because we need a big God.

FEBRUARY 12

We throw open our doors to God and discover at the same moment that he has already thrown open his door to us. We find ourselves standing where we always hoped we might stand—out in the wide open spaces of God's grace and glory, standing tall and shouting our praise.

ROMANS 5:2 THE MESSAGE

# NOVEMBER 19

God is the "One who is" and the "One who causes." And if God is the "One who is," then he is an unchanging God.

FEBRUARY 13

Goodness and mercy. Not goodness alone, for we are sinners in need of mercy. Not mercy alone, for we are fragile, in need of goodness. We need them both. As one man wrote, "Goodness to supply every want. Mercy to forgive every sin. Goodness to provide. Mercy to pardon."

NOVEMBER 18

When we say "I am," we always add another word. "I am happy." "I am sad." "I am strong." "I am Max." God, however, starkly states, "I am" and adds nothing else. "You are what?" we want to ask. "I am," he replies. God needs no descriptive word because he never changes. God is what he is. He is what he has always been.

FEBRUARY 14

And what follows the word surely? "Goodness and mercy." If the Lord is the Shepherd who leads the flock, goodness and mercy are the two sheepdogs that guard the rear of the flock.

NOVEMBER 17

God's immutability motivated the psalmist to declare, "But thou art the same" (Psalm 102:27 KJV). The writer is saying, "You are the One who is. You never change." Yahweh is an unchanging God.

FEBRUARY 15

He is a sure God. And because he is a sure God, we can state confidently, "Surely goodness and mercy shall follow me all the days of my life."

NOVEMBER 16

Yahweh is an uncaused God. Though he creates, God was never created. Though he makes, he was never made. Though he causes, he was never caused. Hence the psalmist's proclamation: "Before the mountains were born or you brought forth the earth and the world, from everlasting to everlasting you are God" (Psalm 90:2 NIV).

FEBRUARY 16

Our moods may shift, but God's doesn't. Our minds may change, but God's doesn't. Our devotion may falter, but God's never does. Even if we are faithless, he is faithful, for he cannot betray himself (2 Timothy 2:13).

# November 15

God is Yahweh—an unchanging God, an uncaused God, and an ungoverned God.

FEBRUARY 17

David would have loved the words of one of his great-great-grandsons, the apostle James. He described God as the one "with whom there is never the slightest variation or shadow of inconsistency" (James 1:17 PHILLIPS).

NOVEMBER 14

Our God gives you everything you need, makes you everything you're to be.

2 THESSALONIANS 1:2 THE MESSAGE

FEBRUARY 18

Open your mouth and taste, open your eyes and see—how good God is. Blessed are you who run to him. Worship God if you want the best; worship opens doors to all his goodness.

PSALM 34:8-9 THE MESSAGE

# NOVEMBER 13

God—our Shepherd—doesn't check the weather; he makes it. He doesn't defy gravity; he created it. He isn't affected by health; he has no body. Jesus said, "God is spirit" (John 4:24).

FEBRUARY 19

David didn't say, "Maybe goodness and mercy shall follow me." Or "Possibly goodness and mercy shall follow me." Or "I have a hunch that goodness and mercy shall follow me." David could have used one of those phrases. But he didn't. He believed in a sure God, who makes sure promises and provides a sure foundation.

NOVEMBER 12

Since God has no body, he has no limitations—equally active in Cambodia as he is in Connecticut. "Where can I go to get away from your Spirit?" asked David. "Where can I run from you? If I go up to the heavens, you are there. If I lie down in the grave, you are there" (Psalm 139:7–8).

# FEBRUARY 20

This must be one of the sweetest phrases ever penned. "Your beauty and love chase after me every day of my life. I'm back home in the house of Yahweh for the rest of my life" (Psalm 23:6 THE MESSAGE). To read the verse is to open a box of jewels. Each word sparkles and begs to be examined in the face of our doubts: goodness, mercy, all the days, dwell in the house of the Lord, forever.

# NOVEMBER 11

Unchanging. Uncaused. Ungoverned. These are only a fraction of God's qualities, but aren't they enough to give you a glimpse of your Father? Don't we need this kind of Shepherd? Don't we need an unchanging Shepherd?

FEBRUARY 21

How does God deal with our doubts? He follows us. He pursues us until we finally see him as our Father, even if it takes all the days of our lives.

*Surely goodness and mercy shall follow me all the days of my life; and I will dwell in the house of the Lord forever.*

PSALM 23:6 NKJV

# NOVEMBER 10

Haven't you had enough change in your life? Relationships change. Health changes. The weather changes. But the Yahweh who ruled the earth last night is the same Yahweh who rules it today. Same convictions. Same plan. Same mood. Same love. He never changes.

Rest from envy. Why? Because your cup overflows.

November 9

You can no more alter God than a pebble can alter the rhythm of the Pacific. Yahweh is a still point in a turning world. Don't we need a still point? Don't we need an unchanging Shepherd?

FEBRUARY 23

One thing is certain. When the final storm comes and you are safe in your Father's house, you won't regret what he didn't give. You'll be stunned at what he did.

N O V E M B E R   8

We need an uncaused Shepherd. No one breathed life into Yahweh. No one sired him. No one gave birth to him. No one caused him. No act brought him forth. And since no act brought him forth, no act can take him out. Does he fear an earthquake? Does he tremble at a tornado? Hardly. Yahweh sleeps through storms and calms the winds with a word.

FEBRUARY 24

Hasn't our Father given us a safe passage and a safe place? A strong wall of grace to protect us? A sure exit to deliver us? Of whom can we be envious? Who has more than we do? Rather than want what others have, shouldn't we wonder if they have what we do? Instead of being jealous of them, how about zealous for them? For heaven's sake, drop the rifles and hold out the cup. There is enough to go around.

NOVEMBER 7

Because of the Lord's great love we are not consumed, for his compassions never fail. They are new every morning; great is your faithfulness.... The Lord is good to those whose hope is in him, to the one who seeks him.

LAMENTATIONS 3:22-23, 25 NIV

# FEBRUARY 25

If God gives such attention to the appearance of wildflowers—
most of which are never even seen—don't you think he'll attend
to you, take pride in you, do his best for you? What I'm trying
to do here is to get you to relax, to not be so preoccupied with
getting, so you can respond to God's giving.

MATTHEW 6:30-31 THE MESSAGE

# NOVEMBER 6

Cancer does not trouble Yahweh, and cemeteries do not disturb him. He was here before they came. He'll be here after they are gone. He is uncaused. And he is ungoverned.

FEBRUARY 26

Have you noticed how wet your table is? God wants you to stay. Your cup overflows with joy. Overflows with grace. Shouldn't your heart overflow with gratitude?

NOVEMBER 5

Counselors can comfort you in the storm, but you need a God who can still the storm.

The overflowing cup was a powerful symbol in the days of David. Hosts in the ancient East used it to send a message to the guest. As long as the cup was kept full, the guest knew he was welcome. But when the cup sat empty, the host was hinting that the hour was late. On those occasions, however, when the host really enjoyed the company of the person, he filled the cup to overflowing. He didn't stop when the wine reached the rim; he kept pouring until the liquid ran over the edge of the cup and down on the table.

# NOVEMBER 4

Friends can hold your hand at your deathbed, but you need a Yahweh who has defeated the grave.

FEBRUARY 28

God gives hope. So what if someone was born thinner or stronger, lighter or darker than you? Why count diplomas or compare résumés? What does it matter if they have a place at the head table? You have a place at God's table. And he is filling your cup to overflowing.

# November 3

Philosophers can debate the meaning of life, but you need a Lord who can declare the meaning of life. You need a Yahweh.

FEBRUARY 29

Surprise us with love at daybreak;
    then we'll skip and dance all the day long....
Let your servants see what you're best at—
    the ways you rule and bless your children.
And let the loveliness of our Lord, our God, rest on us,
    confirming the work that we do.

PSALM 90:14,16-17 THE MESSAGE

# NOVEMBER 2

You don't need to carry the burden of a lesser god...a god on a shelf, a god in a box, or a god in a bottle. No, you need a God who can place 100 billion stars in our galaxy and 100 billion galaxies in the universe. You need a God who can shape two fists of flesh into 75 to 100 billion nerve cells, each with as many as 10,000 connections to other nerve cells, place it in a skull, and call it a brain.

MARCH 1

Just as light pours into a darkened cellar, God's hope pours into your world. Upon the sick, he shines the ray of healing. To the bereaved, he gives the promise of reunion. For the dying, he lit the flame of resurrection. To the confused, he offers the light of Scripture.

# NOVEMBER 1

You need a God who, while so mind-numbingly mighty, can come in the soft of night and touch you with the tenderness of an April snow. You need a Yahweh. And, according to David, you have one. He is your Shepherd.

MARCH 2

Because God pardons you, your cup overflows with hope. "God will help you overflow with hope in him through the Holy Spirit's power within you" (Romans 15:13 TLB).

# OCTOBER 31

Rest from the burden of a small god. Why? Because you have found the Lord.

MARCH 3

God is not a miser with his grace. Your cup may be low on cash or clout, but it is overflowing with mercy. You may not have the prime parking place, but you have sufficient pardon. "He will abundantly pardon" (Isaiah 55:7 NKJV). Your cup overflows with grace.

OCTOBER 30

We humans want to do things our way. Forget the easy way. Forget the common way. Forget the best way. Forget God's way. We want to do things our way. And, according to the Bible, that's precisely our problem. "We all have wandered away like sheep; each of us has gone his own way" (Isaiah 53:6).

MARCH 4

"Can God forgive someone like me?" The answer to this and our questions is found in a letter he wrote to Timothy: "The grace of our Lord was poured out on me abundantly, along with the faith and love that are in Christ Jesus" (1 Timothy 1:14 NIV).

OCTOBER 29

Everyone stops when the ambassador speaks. Everyone listens when God's minstrel sings. Everyone applauds when God's warrior passes. But who notices when God's sheep show up? Who notices when the sheep sing or speak or act? Only one person notices. The Shepherd. And that is precisely David's point. "The Lord is my shepherd."

# MARCH 5

Should the Christian worry that the cup of mercy will run empty? He may. For he may not be aware of God's abounding grace. Are you? Are you aware that the cup God gives you overflows with mercy? Or are you afraid your cup will run dry? Your warranty will expire? Are you afraid your mistakes are too great for God's grace?

OCTOBER 28

But as for me, I watch in hope for the Lord, I wait for God my Savior; my God will hear me.

MICAH 7:7 NIV

# MARCH 6

You're blessed when you care. At the moment of being "care-full," you find yourselves cared for. You're blessed when you get your inside world—your mind and heart—put right. Then you can see God in the outside world.

MATTHEW 5:7-8 THE MESSAGE

OCTOBER 27

When David, who was a warrior, minstrel, and ambassador for God, searched for an illustration of God, he remembered his days as a shepherd. He remembered how he lavished attention on the sheep day and night. How he slept with them and watched over them. And the way he cared for the sheep reminded him of the way God cares for us. David rejoiced to say, "The Lord is my shepherd," and in so doing he proudly implied, "I am his sheep."

# MARCH 7

The blessing of abounding grace. "The more we see our sinfulness, the more we see God's abounding grace forgiving us" (Romans 5:20 TLB). To abound is to have a surplus, an abundance, an extravagant portion. Should the fish in the Pacific worry that it will run out of ocean? No. Why? The ocean abounds with water. Need the lark be anxious about finding room in the sky to fly? No. The sky abounds with space.

# OCTOBER 26

Let's evaluate this. You can't control your moods. A few of your relationships are shaky. You have fears and faults. Hmmm. Do you really want to hang on to your chest of self-reliance? Sounds to me as if you could use a Shepherd.

MARCH 8

The last thing we need to worry about is not having enough. Our cup overflows with blessings.

OCTOBER 25

Rest from doing things your way. Why? Because the Lord is my Shepherd.

MARCH 9

There is no grudging in God's benevolence; He does not measure out his goodness as an apothecary counts his drops and measures his drams, slowly and exactly, drop by drop. God's way is always characterized by multitudinous and overflowing bounty.

F. B. MEYER

OCTOBER 24

Are you in prison? You are if you feel better when you have more and worse when you have less. You are if joy is one delivery away, one transfer away, one award away, or one makeover away. If your happiness comes from something you deposit, drive, drink, or digest, then face it—you are in prison, the prison of want.

MARCH 10

Whatever the blessing is in our cup, it is sure to run over. With him the calf is always the fatted calf; the robe is always the best robe; the joy is unspeakable; the peace passeth understanding.

F. B. MEYER

OCTOBER 23

The good news is, you have a visitor in your prison. And your visitor has a message that can get you paroled. Make your way to the receiving room. Take your seat in the chair, and look across the table at the psalmist David. He motions for you to lean forward. "I have a secret to tell you," he whispers, "the secret of satisfaction. 'The Lord is my shepherd; I shall not want'" (Psalm 23:1 NKJV).

MARCH 11

God's blessing makes life rich; nothing we do can improve on God.

PROVERBS 19:22 THE MESSAGE

OCTOBER 22

All that stuff—it's not yours. And you know what else about all that stuff? It's not you. Who you are has nothing to do with the clothes you wear or the car you drive. Jesus said, "Life is not defined by what you have, even when you have a lot" (Luke 12:15 THE MESSAGE). Heaven does not know you as the fellow with the nice suit or the woman with the big house or the kid with the new bike.

MARCH 12

Is an overflowing cup full? Absolutely. The wine reaches the rim and then tumbles over the edge. The goblet is not large enough to contain the quantity. According to David, our hearts are not large enough to contain the blessings that God wants to give. He pours and pours until they literally flow over the edge and down on the table.

OCTOBER 21

Heaven knows your heart. "The Lord does not look at the things man looks at. Man looks at the outward appearance, but the Lord looks at the heart" (1 Samuel 16:7 NIV).

MARCH 13

Need a deterrent for envy? An antidote for jealousy? The psalm we are studying offers one. Rather than bemoan what you don't have, rejoice in the abundant cup you do.

*My cup overflows with blessings.*

PSALM 23:5 NLT

# OCTOBER 20

When God thinks of you, he may see your compassion, your devotion, your tenderness or quick mind, but he doesn't think of the things you have.

MARCH 14

Rest from my disappointments. Why? Because God anoints me.

O C T O B E R   19

O Lord God Almighty, who is like you?... Righteousness and justice are the foundation of your throne; love and faithfulness go before you.

PSALM 89:8,14 NIV

MARCH 15

Father, help me trust you more to watch over me when I'm feeling alone. And thank you for all the days you stepped into my life, without my even knowing.

*Faith means...knowing that something is real even if we do not see it.*

HEBREWS 11:1

# OCTOBER 18

When you think of you, you shouldn't think of your things. Define yourself by your stuff, and you'll feel good when you have a lot and bad when you don't. Contentment comes when we can honestly say with Paul: "I have learned to be satisfied with the things I have.... I know how to live when I am poor, and I know how to live when I have plenty" (Philippians 4:11–12).

MARCH 16

You were never alone. Only eternity will reveal the time God flattened your tire, preventing you from checking into the hotel and meeting a seductive man or placed the right voice with the right message on the right radio station the day you needed his encouragement.

OCTOBER 17

Are you hoping that a change in circumstances will bring a change in your attitude? If so, you are in prison, and you need to learn a secret of traveling light. What you have in your Shepherd is greater than what you don't have in life.

MARCH 17

The ways of right-living people glow with light; the longer they live, the brighter they shine.... Keep vigilant watch over your heart; that's where life starts.

PROVERBS 4:18,23 THE MESSAGE

# OCTOBER 16

You have a God who hears you, the power of love behind you, the Holy Spirit within you, and all of heaven ahead of you.

MARCH 18

God has been with you all the way. Oh, sometimes you hardly noticed. Only when you get home will you know how many times he protected you. Only eternity will reveal the time he interfered with the transfer, protecting you from involvement in unethical business or fogged in the airport, distancing you from a shady opportunity.

OCTOBER 15

If you have the Shepherd, you have grace for every sin, direction for every turn, a candle for every corner, and an anchor for every storm. You have everything you need.

MARCH 19

So you think you're alone? You think no one cares or no one notices? Someday, when you reach eternity, you may be surprised to learn that you were never alone.

OCTOBER 14

You and I could pray like the Puritan. He sat down to a meal of bread and water. He bowed his head and declared, "All this and Jesus too?"

MARCH 20

We go to God. We bow before him, and we trust in him. The sheep doesn't understand why the oil repels the flies. The sheep doesn't understand how the oil heals the wounds. In fact, all the sheep knows is that something happens in the presence of the shepherd. And that's all we need to know as well.

*Lord, I give myself to you; my God, I trust you.*

PSALM 25:1–2

# OCTOBER 13

Paul says that "godliness with contentment is great gain" (1 Timothy 6:6 niv). When we surrender to God the cumbersome sack of discontent, we don't just give up something; we gain something. God replaces it with a lightweight, tailor-made, sorrow-resistant attaché of gratitude.

MARCH 21

When we come to God, we make requests; we don't make demands. We come with high hopes and a humble heart. We state what we want, but we pray for what is right. And if God gives us the prison of Rome instead of the mission of Spain, we accept it because we know "God will always give what is right to his people who cry to him night and day, and he will not be slow to answer them" (Luke 18:7).

# OCTOBER 12

What will you gain with contentment? You may gain your marriage. You may gain precious hours with your children. You may gain your self-respect. You may gain joy. You may gain the faith to say, "The Lord is my shepherd; I shall not want."

In order to be anointed, the sheep must stand still, lower their heads, and let the shepherd do his work. Peter urges us to "be humble under God's powerful hand so he will lift you up when the right time comes" (1 Peter 5:6).

# OCTOBER 11

Rest from endless wants. Why? Because you shall not want.

MARCH 23

Maybe you don't want to trouble God with your hurts. After all, he's got famines and pestilence and wars; he won't care about my little struggles, you think. Why don't you let him decide that? He cared enough about a wedding to provide the wine. He cared enough about Peter's tax payment to give him a coin. He cared enough about the woman at the well to give her answers. "He cares about you" (1 Peter 5:7).

OCTOBER 10

We are eternal creatures, and we ask eternal questions: Where did I come from? Where am I going? What is the meaning of life? What is right? What is wrong? Is there life after death? These are the primal questions of the soul. And left unanswered, such questions will steal our rest.

MARCH 24

Father, thank you for being my Father, and for loving and comforting me.

*We belong to him; we are his people, the sheep he tends.*

PSALM 100:3

# OCTOBER 9

For sheep to sleep, everything must be just right.
No predators. No tension in the flock. No bugs in the air.
No hunger in the belly. Everything has to be just so.

Have you taken your disappointments to God? You've shared them with your neighbor, your relatives, your friends. But have you taken them to God? James says, "Anyone who is having troubles should pray" (James 5:13). Before you go anywhere else with your disappointments, go to God.

OCTOBER 8

Unfortunately, sheep cannot find safe pasture. They need help. They need a Shepherd to "lead them" and help them "lie down in green pastures." Without a Shepherd, they can't rest.

MARCH 26

Trust God from the bottom of your heart; don't try to figure out everything on your own. Listen for God's voice in everything you do, everywhere you go; he's the one who will keep you on track.

PROVERBS 3:5-6 THE MESSAGE

OCTOBER 7

Do not let your hearts be troubled. Trust in God; trust also in me.... I am going there to prepare a place for you. And if I go and prepare a place for you, I will come back and take you to be with me that you also may be where I am.

JOHN 14:1-3 NIV

MARCH 27

Others may guide us to God. Others may help us understand God. But no one does the work of God, for only God can heal. God "heals the brokenhearted" (Psalm 147:3).

A still pond on one side, the watching Shepherd on the other. "He makes me to lie down in green pastures; He leads me beside the still waters" (Psalm 23:2 NKJV). Note the two pronouns preceding the two verbs. He makes me.... He leads me....  Who is the active one? Who is in charge?

Go to God. David would trust his wounds to no other person but God. He said, "You anoint my head with oil." Not, "your prophets," "your teachers," or "your counselors."

OCTOBER 5

The Shepherd. The Shepherd selects the trail and prepares the pasture. The sheep's job—our job—is to watch the Shepherd. "He leads me" the psalmist reminds us.

MARCH 29

Jesus heals. He touched the broken heart of Mary Magdalene. He touched the confused heart of Cleopas. And he touched the stubborn heart of Paul and the repentant heart of Peter. Jesus tends to his sheep. And he will tend to you.

OCTOBER 4

With our eyes on our Shepherd, we'll be able to get some sleep. "You will keep him in perfect peace, whose mind is stayed on You" (Isaiah 26:3 NKJV).

# MARCH 30

Not only did Jesus prevent wounds, he healed them. He touched the eyes of the blind man. He touched the disease of the leper. He touched the body of the dead girl. Jesus tends to his sheep. He touched the searching heart of Nicodemus. He touched the open heart of Zacchaeus.

OCTOBER 3

We see the waves of the water rather than the Savior walking through them. We focus on our paltry provisions rather than on the One who can feed five thousand hungry people. We concentrate on the dark Fridays of crucifixion and miss the bright Sundays of resurrection. Change your focus and relax. And while you are at it, change your schedule and rest!

# MARCH 31

If the Gospels teach us anything, they teach us that Jesus is a Good Shepherd. "I am the good shepherd," Jesus announces. "The good shepherd gives his life for the sheep" (John 10:11).

OCTOBER 2

You're all I want in heaven! You're all I want on earth!...
I'm in the very presence of God—oh, how refreshing it is!

PSALM 73:25,28 THE MESSAGE

APRIL 1

What a stack of blessing you have
　　　piled up for those who worship you,
Ready and waiting for all who run to you....
　　　You hide them safely away.

PSALM 31:19-20 THE MESSAGE

# OCTOBER 1

"In six days the Lord made the heavens and the earth, the sea, and all that is in them, and rested the seventh day." God's message is plain: "If creation didn't crash when I rested, it won't crash when you do." Repeat these words after me: It is not my job to run the world.

APRIL 2

We, like the sheep, get wounded. And we, like the sheep, have a shepherd. Remember the words we read? "We belong to him; we are his people, the sheep he tends" (Psalm 100:3). Jesus will do for you what the shepherd does for the sheep. He will tend to you.

SEPTEMBER 30

A century ago Charles Spurgeon gave this advice to his preaching students: "Even beasts of burden must be turned out to grass occasionally; the very sea pauses at ebb and flood; earth keeps the Sabbath of the wintry months; and man, even when exalted to God's ambassador, must rest or faint, must trim his lamp or let it burn low; must recruit his vigor or grow prematurely old.... In the long run we shall do more by sometimes doing less."

APRIL 3

Rest from shame. Why? Because God has prepared a place for you in the presence of your enemies.

# SEPTEMBER 29

The bow cannot always be bent without fear of breaking. For a field to bear fruit, it must occasionally lie fallow. And for you to be healthy, you must rest. Slow down, and God will heal you. He will bring rest to your mind, to your body, and most of all to your soul. He will lead you to green pastures.

# APRIL 4

And if any doubt remains, lest there be any "Peters" who wonder if there is a place at the table for them, Jesus issues a tender reminder as he passes the cup. "Every one of you drink this. This is my blood which is the new agreement that God makes with his people. This blood is poured out for many to forgive their sins" (Matthew 26:27–28). "Every one of you drink this." Those who feel unworthy, drink this. Those who feel ashamed, drink this. Those who feel embarrassed, drink this.

# SEPTEMBER 28

Green pastures were not the natural terrain of Judea. The hills around Bethlehem where David kept his flock were not lush and green. Even today they are white and parched. Any green pasture in Judea is the work of some shepherd. Jesus has created a pasture for our souls. And he invites us to rest there. Can you imagine the satisfaction in the heart of the Shepherd when, with work completed, he sees his sheep rest in the tender grass?

APRIL 5

What if your Shepherd did for you what the shepherd did for his flock? Suppose he dealt with your enemy, the devil, and prepared for you a safe place of nourishment? What if Jesus did for you what he did for Peter? Suppose he, in the hour of your failure, invited you to a meal?

# SEPTEMBER 27

With his own pierced hands, Jesus created a pasture for the soul. He tore out the thorny underbrush of condemnation. He pried loose the huge boulders of sin. In their place he planted seeds of grace and dug ponds of mercy.

APRIL 6

And the rooster crows, and conviction pierces, and Peter has a partner in the shadows. We weep as Peter wept, and we do what Peter did. We go fishing. We go back to our old lives. We return to our pre-Jesus practices. We do what comes naturally, rather than what comes spiritually. And we question whether Jesus has a place for folks like us.

*You didn't choose me, remember; I chose you.*

JOHN 15:13 THE MESSAGE

# SEPTEMBER 26

The pasture Jesus created is his gift to us. This is not a pasture that you have made. Nor is it a pasture that you deserve. It is a gift of God. "For it is by grace you have been saved, through faith—and this not from yourselves, it is the gift of God" (Ephesians 2:8 NIV).

APRIL 7

Christ had returned, but Peter wondered, he must have wondered, "After what I did, would he return for someone like me?" We've wondered the same. Is Peter the only person to do the very thing he swore he'd never do?

*Just then a rooster crowed. Peter remembered what Jesus had said: "Before the rooster crows, you will deny me three times." He went out and cried and cried and cried.*

MATTHEW 26:75 THE MESSAGE

# SEPTEMBER 25

In a world rocky with human failure, there is a land lush with divine mercy. Your Shepherd invites you there. He wants you to lie down. Nestle deeply until you are hidden, buried, in the tall shoots of his love, and there you will find rest.

A P R I L   8

Rest from loneliness. Why? Because God is with you.

SEPTEMBER 24

Are you tired? Worn out? Burned out on religion? Come to me. Get away with me and you'll recover your life. I'll show you how to take a real rest. Walk with me and work with me—watch how I do it. Learn the unforced rhythms of grace. I won't lay anything heavy or ill-fitting on you. Keep company with me and you'll learn to live freely and lightly.

MATTHEW 11:28-30 THE MESSAGE

APRIL 9

Father, help me understand and accept that a lonely season can bring me closer to you.

*Delight yourself in the Lord and he will give you the desires of your heart.*

PSALM 37:4 NIV

# SEPTEMBER 23

Rest from weariness. Why? Because God makes me to lie down.

# APRIL 10

Loneliness. Could it be one of God's finest gifts? If a season of solitude is his way to teach you to hear his song, don't you think it's worth it? So do I.

SEPTEMBER 22

Worry is the burlap bag of burdens. Cumbersome. Chunky. Unattractive. Scratchy. Hard to get a handle on. Irritating to carry and impossible to give away. No one wants your worries. Sadly, worrying is one job you can't farm out, but you can overcome it. There is no better place to begin than "beside the still waters," where the Shepherd leads.

APRIL 11

For fear of going unnoticed, we dress to seduce or to impress. For fear of sleeping alone, we sleep with anyone. For fear of not being loved, we search for love in all the wrong places. But God's love is perfect. And, "perfect love casts out fear" (1 John 4:18 NKJV).

# SEPTEMBER 21

No one has to remind you of the high cost of anxiety. Worry divides the mind. The biblical word for worry (merimnao) is a compound of two Greek words, merizo (to divide) and nous (the mind). Anxiety splits our energy between today's priorities and tomorrow's problems. Part of our mind is on the now; the rest is on the not yet. The result is half-minded living.

APRIL 12

Why do we try to buy things we don't need? Because we fear facing life alone. For fear of not fitting in, we take the drugs. For fear of standing out, we wear the clothes. For fear of appearing small, we go into debt and buy the house. But all that changes when we discover God's perfect love.

SEPTEMBER 20

Anxiety is an expensive habit. Of course, it might be worth the cost if it worked. But it doesn't. Our frets are futile. Jesus said, "You cannot add any time to your life by worrying about it" (Matthew 6:27). Worry has never brightened a day, solved a problem, or cured a disease.

A P R I L  13

What a wildly wonderful world, God! You made it all, with Wisdom at your side, made earth overflow with your wonderful creations.

PSALM 104:24 THE MESSAGE

# SEPTEMBER 19

"He leads me beside the still waters," David declares. And, in case we missed the point, he repeats the phrase in the next verse: "He leads me in the paths of righteousness."

APRIL 14

Your family may turn against you, but God won't. Your friends may betray you, but God won't. You may feel alone in the wilderness, but you are not. He is with you. And because he is, everything is different. You are different. When you know God loves you, you won't be desperate for the love of others.

SEPTEMBER 18

"He leads me." God isn't behind me, yelling, "Go!" He is ahead of me, bidding, "Come!" He is in front, clearing the path, cutting the brush, showing the way. Just before the curve, he says, "Turn here." Prior to the rise, he motions, "Step up here." Standing next to the rocks, he warns, "Watch your step here."

APRIL 15

Father, your presence enriches my days. Thank you for walking with me through the lonely times of life.

*Be still before the Lord and wait patiently for him.*

PSALM 37:7 NIV

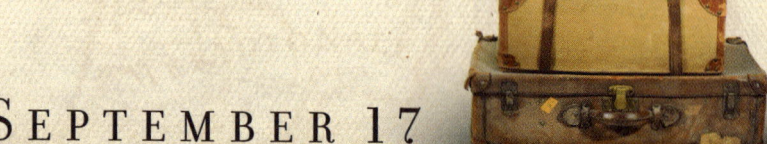

# SEPTEMBER 17

God leads us. He tells us what we need to know when we need to know it. As a New Testament writer would affirm: "We will find grace to help us when we need it" (Hebrews 4:16 NLT).

# APRIL 16

You may be facing marital struggles, but you aren't facing them alone; the Lord is with you. You may be facing debt, but you aren't facing debt alone; the Lord is with you. Underline these words: You are not alone.

SEPTEMBER 16

"Let us therefore boldly approach the throne of our gracious God, where we may receive mercy and in his grace find timely help" (Hebrews 4:16 NEB).

# APRIL 17

God wants you to discover what David discovered and to be able to say what David said. "You are with me." Yes, you, Lord, are in heaven. Yes, you rule the universe. Yes, you sit upon the stars and make your home in the deep. But yes, yes, yes, you are with me. The Lord is with me. The Creator is with me. Yahweh is with me.

SEPTEMBER 15

We all live off his generous bounty,
gift after gift after gift....
this exuberant giving and receiving,
This endless knowing and understanding–
all this came through Jesus, the Messiah.

JOHN 1:16-17 THE MESSAGE

APRIL 18

A friend turns away. The job goes bad. Your spouse doesn't understand. The church is dull. One by one he removes the options until all you have left is God. He would do that? Absolutely. "The Lord disciplines those he loves" (Hebrews 12:6). If he must silence every voice, he will. He wants you to hear his music.

SEPTEMBER 14

God's help is timely. He places himself between you and the need. And at the right time, he gives you what you need.

APRIL 19

Yes, you, Lord, are in heaven. Yes, you rule the universe. Yes, you sit upon the stars and make your home in the deep. But yes, yes, yes, you are with me. Father, when I feel lonely, remind me of your presence. Let me know that you are with me.

*You are with me.*

PSALM 23:4 NKJV

# SEPTEMBER 13

Wasn't timely help the promise Jesus gave his disciples? "When you are arrested and judged, don't worry ahead of time about what you should say. Say whatever is given you to say at that time, because it will not really be you speaking; it will be the Holy Spirit" (Mark 13:11).

APRIL 20

Oh, how God wants you to hear his music. He has a rhythm that will race your heart and lyrics that will stir your tears. You want to journey to the stars? He can take you there. You want to lie down in peace? His music can soothe your soul.

SEPTEMBER 12

Isn't timely help the message God gave the children of Israel? He promised to supply them with manna each day. But he told them to collect only one day's supply at a time. Those who disobeyed and collected enough for two days found themselves with rotten manna. The only exception to the rule was the day prior to the Sabbath. On Friday they could gather twice as much. Otherwise, God would give them what they needed, in their time of need.

# APRIL 21

I've learned by now to be quite content whatever my circumstances. I'm just as happy with little as with much, with much as with little.... Whatever I have, wherever I am, I can make it through anything in the One who makes me who I am.

PHILIPPIANS 4:11-13 THE MESSAGE

# SEPTEMBER 11

God leads us. God will do the right thing at the right time. And what a difference that makes.

APRIL 22

We'll try anything to unload our loneliness. This is one bag we want to drop quickly. But should we be so quick to drop it? Could it be that loneliness is not a curse but a gift? A gift from God? Loneliness is anything but a gift. But I wonder if loneliness is God's way of getting our attention.

# September 10

Since I know his provision is timely, I can enjoy the present.

APRIL 23

Bags of loneliness show up everywhere. They litter the floors of boardrooms and clubs. We drag them into parties and usually drag them back out. You'll spot them near the desk of the overworker, beside the table of the overeater, and on the nightstand of the one-night stand.

SEPTEMBER 9

The key is this: Meet today's problems with today's strength. Don't start tackling tomorrow's problems until tomorrow. You do not have tomorrow's strength yet. You simply have enough for today.

APRIL 24

Loneliness is not the absence of faces. It is the absence of intimacy. Loneliness doesn't come from being alone; it comes from feeling alone. Whether it strikes you in your bed at night or on your drive to the hospital, in the silence of an empty house or the noise of a crowded bar, loneliness is when you think, I feel so alone. Does anyone care?

*God is love.... This is love: not that we loved God, but that he loved us.*

I JOHN 4:8, 10 NIV

# SEPTEMBER 8

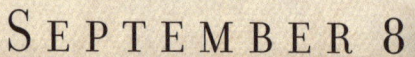

Give your entire attention to what God is doing right now, and don't get worked up about what may or may not happen tomorrow. God will help you deal with whatever hard things come up when the time comes.

MATTHEW 6:34 THE MESSAGE

APRIL 25

The discovery of David is indeed the message of Scripture—the Lord is with us. And, since the Lord is near, everything is different. Everything! Lord, be near to me today! I give you this day and rejoice in your promise to make my heart your home.

# SEPTEMBER 7

Each one of you is certainly a much more marvelous organization than that great liner the Titanic and bound on a far longer voyage. What I urge is that you learn to master your life by living each day in a day-tight compartment and this will certainly ensure your safety throughout your entire journey of life.

APRIL 26

Father, when a winter of loneliness comes, I ask you to give me the warmth of your presence.

*Give ear to my words, O Lord, consider my sighing. Listen to my cry for help, my King and my God, for to you I pray.*

PSALM 5:1-2 NIV

# SEPTEMBER 6

Ensure your safety throughout your entire journey of life. Touch a button and hear, at every level of your life, the iron doors shutting out the Past—the dead yesterdays. Touch another and shut off, with a metal curtain, the Future—the unborn tomorrows. Then you are safe—safe for today.

Sir William Osler

# April 27

The Lord is with us. You may be facing death, but you aren't facing death alone; the Lord is with you. You may be facing unemployment, but you aren't facing unemployment alone; the Lord is with you.

SEPTEMBER 5

Think not of the amount to be accomplished, the difficulties to be overcome, but set earnestly at the little task near your elbow, letting that be sufficient for the day; for surely our plain duty is not to see what lies dimly at a distance but to do what lies clearly at hand.

Sir William Osler

April 28

What happens when we live God's way? He brings gifts into our lives, much the same way that fruit appears in an orchard— things like affection for others, exuberance about life, serenity. We develop a willingness to stick with things, a sense of compassion in the heart, and a conviction that a basic holiness permeates things and people.

GALATIANS 5:22-23 THE MESSAGE

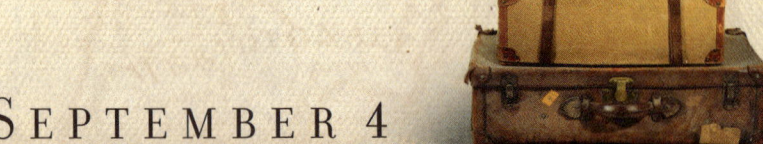

# SEPTEMBER 4

You're blessed when you're content with just who you are—no more, no less. That's the moment you find yourselves proud owners of everything that can't be bought.

MATTHEW 5:5 THE MESSAGE

APRIL 29

Remember the message of Scripture, since the Lord is near, everything is different.

SEPTEMBER 3

Jesus made this point in a few words: "So don't worry about tomorrow, because tomorrow will have its own worries. Each day has enough trouble of its own" (Matthew 6:34). Easy to say. Not always easy to do, right? We are so prone to worry.

APRIL 30

David was no stranger to loneliness. You aren't either. By now you've learned that you don't have to be alone to feel lonely. Two thousand years ago 250 million people populated the earth. Now there are more than 5 billion. If loneliness could be cured by the presence of people, then surely there would be less loneliness today. But loneliness lingers.

SEPTEMBER 2

Just last night I was worrying in my sleep. I dreamed that I was diagnosed with ALS, a degenerative muscle disease, which took the life of my father. I awakened from the dream and, right there in the middle of the night, began to worry. Then Jesus' words came to my mind, "Don't worry about tomorrow." And for once, I decided not to. I dropped the burlap sack. I did the most spiritual thing I could have done. I went back to sleep.

MAY 1

Rest from fear. Why? Because God's presence comforts you.

SEPTEMBER 1

God is leading you. Leave tomorrow's problems until tomorrow.

MAY 2

More significant than any other title or position—is the simple fact that you are God's child. Father, you are my Father, and I will not fear. I know that nothing can separate me from you, and that fact brings great peace.

*What marvelous love the Father has extended to us! Just look at it— we're called children of God! That's who we really are.*

1 John 3:1 THE MESSAGE

# AUGUST 31

Lead, kindly Light...
Keep Thou my feet; I do not ask to see
The distant scene; one step enough for me.

JOHN HENRY NEWMAN

MAY 3

Jesus, at this very moment, is protecting you.... Evil must pass through Christ before it can touch you. And God will "never let you be pushed past your limit; he'll always be there to help you come through it" (1 Corinthians 10:13 THE MESSAGE). Just knowing that helps dispel fear, doesn't it? Lord, thank you for bringing calm to the storms of my fears.

AUGUST 30

God isn't going to let you see the distant scene either. So you might as well quit looking for it. He promises a lamp unto our feet, not a crystal ball into the future. We do not need to know what will happen tomorrow. We only need to know he leads us and "we will find grace to help us when we need it" (Hebrews 4:16 NLT).

MAY 4

Jesus is praying for us.... Jesus has spoken and Satan has listened. The devil may land a punch or two. He may even win a few rounds, but he never wins the fight. Why? Because Jesus takes up for you.... "So he is able always to save those who come to God through him because he always lives, asking God to help them" (Hebrews 7:25).

AUGUST 29

Rest from worry. Why? Because God leads you.

M A Y  5

Father, I'm looking to you and asking you to calm my fears, trusting that you will do what is best and what is right.

*Surely God is my salvation; I will trust and not be afraid.*

ISAIAH 12:2 NIV

# AUGUST 28

Can you sense, for just a second, how it feels to be out of your element? Out of solutions? Out of ideas and energy? Can you imagine, just for a moment, how it feels to be out of hope? If you can, you can relate to many people in this world.

MAY 6

Instead of carrying the world on your shoulders, talk to the One who holds the universe on his. Hope is a look away. Now, what were you looking at?

AUGUST 27

He heals the heartbroken.... He counts the stars and assigns each a name. Our Lord is great, with limitless strength; we'll never comprehend what he knows and does.

PSALM 147:3-5 THE MESSAGE

MAY 7

"Do not be anxious about anything, but in everything, by prayer and petition, with thanksgiving, present your requests to God" (Philippians 4:6 NIV). Don't measure the size of the mountain; talk to the One who can move it.

# AUGUST 26

For many people, life is—well, life is a jungle. Not a jungle of trees and beasts. Would that it were so simple. Would that our jungles could be cut with a machete or our adversaries trapped in a cage. But our jungles are comprised of the thicker thickets of failing health, broken hearts, and empty wallets.

# MAY 8

God knows what you need. That's why we punctuate our prayers as Jesus did. "If you are willing…" Was God willing? Yes and no. He didn't take away the cross, but he took the fear. God didn't still the storm, but he calmed the sailor.

AUGUST 25

We don't hear the screeching of birds or the roaring of lions, but we do hear the complaints of neighbors and the demands of bosses. Our predators are our creditors, and the brush that surrounds us is the rush that exhausts us. It's a jungle out there.

MAY 9

Father, I am fearful, but I know that you are strong when I am weak. Help me sense your presence in the midst of my fear.

*Father, if you are willing, take away this cup of suffering. But do what you want, not what I want.*

LUKE 22:42

# AUGUST 24

What would it take to restore your hope? What would you need to reenergize your journey? When you have no hope, you need some vision. You need someone to lift your spirits. You need someone to look you in the face and say, "This isn't the end. Don't give up. There is a better place than this. And I'll lead you there."

MAY 10

Jesus doesn't think your fears are foolish or silly. He won't tell you to "buck up" or "get tough." He's been where you are. He knows how you feel.

A UGUST 23

When you have no hope, you need direction. If you have only a person but no renewed vision, all you have is company. If he has a vision but no direction, you have a dreamer for company. But if you have a person with direction—who can take you from this place to the right place—ah, then you have one who can restore your hope.

MAY 11

Do what Jesus did in the Garden of Gethsemane; open your heart. And be specific. Jesus was. "Take this cup," he prayed. Give God the number of the flight. Tell him the length of the speech. Share the details of the job transfer. He has plenty of time. He also has plenty of compassion.

AUGUST 22

Our Shepherd majors in restoring hope to the soul. Whether you are a lamb lost on a craggy ledge or a city slicker alone in a deep jungle, everything changes when your rescuer appears.

MAY 12

The words of Psalm 56:3 says "When I am afraid, I put my trust in you" (NLT). Do the same with your fears. Don't avoid life's Gardens of Gethsemane. Enter them. Just don't enter them alone. And while there, be honest. Pounding the ground is permitted. Tears are allowed. And if you sweat blood, you won't be the first.

# AUGUST 21

When your rescuer appears, your loneliness diminishes, because you have fellowship.

MAY 13

Lord, thank you for being my rescuer. Thank you for the assurance that you are watchful, that you care, and that you are my protector.

*May the God you serve all the time save you!*

Daniel 6:16

# August 20

You've always been great toward me—what love!...
You, O God, are both tender and kind,
not easily angered, immense in love,
and you never, never quit.

PSALM 86:13, 15 THE MESSAGE

MAY 14

The counsel of the Hebrew epistle is "looking unto Jesus." What was the focus of David? "You are with me; Your rod and Your staff, they comfort me." How did Jesus endure the terror of the crucifixion? He went first to the Father with his fears.

AUGUST 19

When your rescuer appears, your despair decreases, because you have vision.

MAY 15

Let us run with endurance the race that is set before us,
looking unto Jesus, the author and finisher of our faith.

HEBREWS 12:1–2 NKJV

AUGUST 18

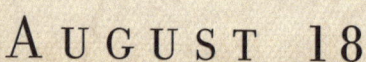

When your rescuer appears, your confusion begins to lift, because you have direction.

MAY 16

Our forerunner is Jesus, the "author and finisher of our faith." He is the author—that is to say he wrote the book on salvation. And he is the finisher—he not only charted the map, he blazed the trail. He is the forerunner, and we are the runners. And we runners are urged to keep our eyes on Jesus.

AUGUST 17

You have hope because you have met someone who can lead you out. Your Shepherd knows that you were not made for this place. He knows you are not equipped for this place. So he has come to guide you out. He has come to restore your soul. He is the perfect one to do so.

MAY 17

Because Jesus knew where to look. "You are with me; Your rod and Your staff, they comfort me." Rather than turn to the other sheep, David turned to the Shepherd. Rather than stare at the problems, he stared at the rod and staff. Because he knew where to look, David was able to say, "I will fear no evil."

AUGUST 16

Your Shepherd has the right vision. He reminds you that "you are like foreigners and strangers in this world" (1 Peter 2:11). And he urges you to lift your eyes from the jungle around you to the heaven above you. "Don't shuffle along, eyes to the ground, absorbed with the things right in front of you. Look up, and be alert to what is going on around Christ.... See things from his perspective" (Colossians 3:2 THE MESSAGE).

MAY 18

We tend to go everywhere else for help. First to the bar, to the counselor, to the self-help book or the friend next door. Not Jesus. The first one to hear his fear was his Father in heaven.

AUGUST 15

David urges you to lift your eyes from the jungle around you: "I lift up my eyes to the hills—where does my help come from? My help comes from the Lord, the Maker of heaven and earth. He will not let your foot slip—he who watches over you will not slumber.... The Lord watches over you... the sun will not harm you by day, nor the moon by night. The Lord will keep you from all harm—he will watch over your life" (Psalm 121:1–7 NIV).

# MAY 19

There is far more to your inner life than the food you put in your stomach, more to your outer appearance than the clothes you hang on your body. Look at the ravens, free and unfettered, not tied down to a job description, carefree in the care of God. And you count far more.

LUKE 12:22-23 THE MESSAGE

# AUGUST 14

God, your rescuer, has the right vision. He also has the right direction. He made the boldest claim in the history of man when he declared, "I am the way" (John 14:6). People wondered if the claim was accurate. He answered their questions by cutting a path through the underbrush of sin and death...and escaping alive. He's the only One who ever did. And he is the only One who can help you and me do the same.

MAY 20

"Father, if you are willing, take away this cup of suffering." The first one to hear Jesus' fear is his Father. He could have gone to his mother. He could have confided in his disciples. He could have assembled a prayer meeting. All would have been appropriate, but none were his priority. He went first to his Father.

God is all mercy and grace—not quick to anger, is rich in love. God is good to one and all; everything he does is suffused with grace.

PSALM 145:8-9 THE MESSAGE

MAY 21

We tend to gloss over our fears. Cover them up. Keep our sweaty palms in our pockets, our nausea and dry mouths a secret. Not so with Jesus. We see no mask of strength. But we do hear his request for strength.

*Father, if you are willing, take this cup from me; yet not my will, but yours be done.*

LUKE 22:42 NIV

# AUGUST 12

Jesus has the right vision: He has seen the homeland. He has the right directions: He has cut the path. But most of all, he is the right person, for he is our God. Who knows the jungle better than the One who made it? And who knows the pitfalls of the path better than the One who has walked it?

MAY 22

Jesus was more than anxious; he was afraid. Fear is worry's big brother. If worry is a burlap bag, fear is a trunk of concrete. It wouldn't budge. How remarkable that Jesus felt such fear. But how kind that he told us about it.

AUGUST 11

The story is told of a man on an African safari deep in the jungle. The guide before him had a machete and was whacking away the tall weeds and thick underbrush. The traveler, wearied and hot, asked in frustration, "Where are we? Do you know where you are taking me? Where is the path?!" The seasoned guide stopped and looked back at the man and replied, "I am the path."

M AY 23

Isn't it likely that fear is one of the emotions Jesus felt? One might even argue that fear was the primary emotion. He saw something in the future so fierce, so foreboding that he begged for a change of plans.

*Father, if you are willing, take away this cup of suffering.*

LUKE 22:42

# AUGUST 10

We ask God, "Where are you taking me? Where is the path?" And he, like a seasoned guide, doesn't tell us. Oh, he may give us a hint or two, but that's all. If he did, would we understand? Would we comprehend our location? No, like a traveler on safari, we are unacquainted with this jungle. So rather than give us an answer, Jesus gives us a far greater gift. He gives us himself.

MAY 24

The gospel of Mark says, "Jesus fell to the ground" (Mark 14:35). Matthew tells us Jesus was "very sad and troubled...to the point of death" (Matthew 26:37–38). According to Luke, Jesus was "full of pain" (Luke 22:44). What do we do with this image of Jesus? Simple. We turn to it when we look the same. We read it when we feel the same; we read it when we feel afraid.

AUGUST 9

Does Jesus give us hope by removing our jungle? No, the vegetation is still thick. Does he purge the predators? No, danger still lurks. Jesus doesn't give hope by changing the jungle; he restores our hope by giving us himself. And he has promised to stay until the very end. "I am with you always, to the very end of the age" (Matthew 28:20 NIV).

# MAY 25

It's the expression of Jesus that puzzles us. We've never seen his face like this. Jesus smiling, yes. Jesus weeping, absolutely. Jesus stern, even that. But Jesus anguished? Cheeks streaked with tears? Face flooded in sweat? Rivulets of blood dripping from his chin? You remember the night.

*Then an angel from heaven appeared to him to strengthen him. Being full of pain, Jesus prayed even harder. His sweat was like drops of blood falling to the ground.*

Luke 22:43-44

# August 8

We need to be reminded that Jesus gives us hope by giving us himself. We all need that reminder. For all of us need hope.

*My Presence will go with you, and I will give you rest.*

Exodus 33:14 NIV

# MAY 26

Rest from the valley of death. Why? Because God walks you through it.

AUGUST 7

You may not need hope right now. Your jungle has become a meadow and your journey a delight. But remember—we do not know what tomorrow holds. We do not know where this road will lead. You may be one turn from a cemetery, from a hospital bed, from an empty house. You may be a bend in the road from a jungle. And though you don't need your hope restored today, you may tomorrow. And you need to know to whom to turn.

MAY 27

We face death, but thanks to Jesus, we only face its shadow. And thanks to Jesus, we believe that our loved ones are happy as they've passed through the valley of the shadow of death.

AUGUST 6

Perhaps you need hope today. You know you were not made for this place. You know you are not equipped. You want someone to lead you out. If so, call out for your Shepherd. He knows your voice. And he's just waiting for your request.

MAY 28

Don't heed, but do forgive, those who urge you not to face, fight, or question death. God will lead you through, not around, the valley of the shadow of death. And, by the way, aren't you glad it's just a shadow?

AUGUST 5

Rest from hopelessness. Why? Because God restores your soul.

Death cannot be soft-pedaled or passed over. Face it, fight it, question it, or condemn it, but don't deny it. As David's son Solomon explained, "There is...a time to mourn" (Ecclesiastes 3:1, 4 NIV).

# AUGUST 4

God is planning a party...a party to end all parties. Not a cookie party, but a feast. Not giggles and chitchat in the conference room, but wide-eyed wonder in the throne room of God.

In God's plan every life is long enough and every death is timely. And though you and I might wish for a longer life, God knows better.

AUGUST 3

God is planning a party...a party to end all parties. And what we now see vaguely, there we will see clearly. We will see God. Not by faith. Not via Scripture or sunsets or summer rains. We will see not God's work or words, but we will see him! For he is not the host of the party; he is the party. His goodness is the banquet. His voice is the music. His radiance is the light, and his love is the endless topic of discussion.

MAY 31

Death is God's way of taking people away from evil. From what kind of evil? An extended disease? An addiction? A dark season of rebellion? We don't know. But we know that no person lives one day more or less than God intends.

*All the days planned for me were written in your book before I was one day old.*

PSALM 139:16

# AUGUST 2

All of us occasionally do what is right. A few predominantly do what is right. But do any of us always do what is right? According to Paul we don't. "There is none righteous, no, not one" (Romans 3:10 NKJV).

# June 1

God does only what is good. But how can death be good? Some mourners don't ask this question. When the quantity of years has outstripped the quality of years, we don't ask how death can be good. Part of the answer may be found in Isaiah 57:1–2: "Good people are taken away, but no one understands. Those who do right are being taken away from evil and are given peace. Those who live as God wants find rest in death."

AUGUST 1

Paul is adamant when he says, "No one anywhere has kept on doing what is right; not one" (Romans 3:12 TLB). Some may beg to differ. "I'm not perfect, Max, but I'm better than most folks. I've led a good life. I don't break the rules. I don't break hearts. I help people. I like people. Compared to others, I think I could say I'm a righteous person."

JUNE 2

Embrace this God-life. Really embrace it, and nothing will be too much for you.... That's why I urge you to pray for absolutely everything, ranging from small to large. Include everything as you embrace this God-life, and you'll get God's everything.

MARK 11:22-24 THE MESSAGE

# JULY 31

God points to himself and says, "This is what I mean by righteousness." Righteousness is who God is. "Our God and Savior Jesus Christ does what is right" (2 Peter 1:1).

JUNE 3

"Taste and see that the Lord is good" (Psalm 34:8 NIV). God is a good God. We must begin here. Though we don't understand his actions, we can trust his heart.

JULY 30

God is righteous. His decrees are righteous. His judgment is righteous. His requirements are righteous. His acts are righteous. Daniel declared, "Our God is right in everything he does."

Only God knows the reasons behind his actions. But here is a key truth on which we can stand. Our God is a good God. "You are good, Lord. The Lord is good and right" (Psalm 25:7–8).

JULY 29

God is never wrong. He has never rendered a wrong decision, experienced the wrong attitude, taken the wrong path, said the wrong thing, or acted the wrong way. He is never too late or too early, too loud or too soft, too fast or too slow. He has always been and always will be right. He is righteous.

JUNE 5

Are you passing through the valley of the shadow? Is this book being held by the same hands that touched the cold face of a friend? And the eyes that fall upon this page, have they also fallen upon the breathless figure of a husband, wife, or child? Are you passing through the valley? You know that the black bag of sorrow is hard to bear.

J U L Y  2 8

You have made known to me the path of life; you will fill me with joy in your presence, with eternal pleasures at your right hand.

PSALM 16:11 NIV

# JUNE 6

The Good Shepherd is with you. And because he is with you, you can say what David said: "I will fear no evil; for You are with me; Your rod and Your staff, they comfort me."

JULY 27

Will God, who is righteous, spend eternity with those who are not? Would Harvard admit a third-grade dropout? If it did, the act might be benevolent, but it wouldn't be right. If God accepted the unrighteous, the invitation would be even nicer, but would he be right? Would he be right to overlook our sins? Lower his standards? No. He wouldn't be right. And if God is anything, he is right.

JUNE 7

What God said to the nation of Israel, he says to you: "When you pass through the waters, I will be with you" (Isaiah 43:2 NIV).

J U L Y   26

God told Isaiah that righteousness would be his plumb line, the standard by which his house is measured (Isaiah 28:17). Paul uses this analogy: "We're sinners, every one of us, in the same sinking boat with everybody else" (Romans 3:19 THE MESSAGE). Then what are we to do?

JUNE 8

What God said to Joshua, he says to you: "As I was with Moses, so I will be with you; I will never leave you nor forsake you" (Joshua 1:5 NIV).

# July 25

Listen. The weight of weariness pulls you down. Self-reliance misleads you. Disappointments discourage you. Anxiety plagues you. But guilt? Guilt consumes you. I can tell you what I did. I confessed my need.

JUNE 9

What God said to Jacob, he says to you: "I am with you and will watch over you wherever you go" (Genesis 28:15 NIV).

# JULY 24

Rather than dismiss our sin, he assumes our sin and, incredibly, sentences himself. God's holiness is honored. Our sin is punished...and we are redeemed. God does what we cannot do so we can be what we dare not dream: perfect before God. Does such a God want his children burdened by sin? I don't think so, either. Lord, thank you for reminding me to focus on your holiness instead of my own guilt.

JUNE 10

What God said to Moses, he says to you: "My Presence will go with you, and I will give you rest" (Exodus 33:14 NIV).

JULY 23

Those who taste God's presence have declared spiritual bankruptcy and are aware of their spiritual crisis.... Their pockets are empty. Their options are gone. They have long since stopped demanding justice; they are pleading for mercy.

# June 11

When God calls us into the deep valley of death, he will be with us. Dare we think that he would abandon us in the moment of death? Would the shepherd require his sheep to journey to the highlands alone? Of course not. Would God require his child to journey to eternity alone? Absolutely not! He is with you!

J U L Y   2 2

Your thoughts—how rare, how beautiful! God, I'll never comprehend them! I couldn't even begin to count them—any more than I could count the sand of the sea. Oh, let me rise in the morning and live always with you!

PSALM 139:17-18 THE MESSAGE

JUNE 12

For God is sheer beauty, all-generous in love, loyal always and ever.

PSALM 100:5 THE MESSAGE

JULY 21

Lord, today I surrender my life, my past, my sins to you. I am nothing without you, Father. And yet, I am everything with you. I praise your holy name for redeeming me.

JUNE 13

"I will come back and take you home." Jesus is your personal Shepherd. And he is personally responsible to lead you home. And because he is present when any one of his sheep dies, you can say what David said, "I will fear no evil."

JULY 20

It was, at once, history's most beautiful and most horrible moment. Jesus stood in the tribunal of heaven. Sweeping a hand over all creation, he pleaded, "Punish me for their mistakes. See the murderer? Give me his penalty. The adulteress? I'll take her shame. The bigot, the liar, the thief? Do to me what you would do to them. Treat me as you would a sinner." And God did.

*For Christ died for sins once for all, the righteous for the unrighteous, to bring you to God.*

1 PETER 3:18 NIV

# JUNE 14

Note the promise of Jesus. "I will come back and take you to be with me." He pledges to take us home. He does not delegate this task. He may send missionaries to teach you, angels to protect you, teachers to guide you, singers to inspire you, and physicians to heal you, but he sends no one to take you. He reserves this job for himself.

JULY 19

Yes, righteousness is what God is, and, yes, righteousness is what we are not, and, yes, righteousness is what God requires. But "God has a way to make people right with him" (Romans 3:21). David said it like this: "He leads me in the paths of righteousness" (Psalm 23:3 NKJV).

# JUNE 15

Years after David wrote these words, another Bethlehem Shepherd would say: "There are many rooms in my Father's house; I would not tell you this if it were not true. I am going there to prepare a place for you. After I go and prepare a place for you, I will come back and take you to be with me so that you may be where I am" (John 14:2–3).

# JULY 18

Guilt doesn't bring us nearer to God; it distances us from him. Listen. Disappointments may discourage you. Anxiety may plague you. But guilt? Guilt consumes you. So what do we do? Confess our need. Proclaim our guilt to the Father. And accept the righteousness of God, freely given by the One whose sacrifice makes us righteous. Father, you are holy and righteous, and I gratefully accept your gift of redemption.

Don't even speak of death without speaking to God. He and he alone can guide you through the valley. Others may speculate or aspire, but only God knows the way to get you home. And only God is committed to getting you there safely.

JULY 17

God's love is meteoric,
    his loyalty astronomic,
His purpose titanic,
    his verdicts oceanic.
Yet in his largeness
    nothing gets lost.

PSALM 36:5-6 THE MESSAGE

# JUNE 17

"You are with me; Your rod and Your staff, they comfort me."
David's implied message is subtle but crucial. Don't face death
without facing God.

JULY 16

The path of righteousness is a narrow, winding trail up a steep hill. At the top of the hill is a cross. At the base of the cross are bags. Countless bags full of innumerable sins. Calvary is the compost pile for guilt. Would you like to leave yours there as well? Father, today I will transfer my burden of guilt to your loving arms. Thank you for leading me on the path of righteousness by taking my guilt.

JUNE 18

David was honest about death. He may have slain Goliath, but he had no illusions about sidestepping the giant of death. And though his first reminder sobers us, his second reminder encourages us: We don't have to face death alone.

JULY 15

We have a Father who is filled with compassion, a Father who hurts when his children hurt. We serve a God who says that even when we stumble, even when we disobey, he is waiting to embrace us and forgive us.

*Where God's love is, there is no fear, because God's perfect love drives out fear.*

1 JOHN 4:18

# JUNE 19

God's a...sanctuary during bad times. The moment you arrive, you relax.

PSALM 9:9-10 THE MESSAGE

JULY 14

In the throne room of God, what we now see vaguely, there we will see clearly. We will see not God's work or words, but we will see him! For he is not the host of the party; he is the party. His goodness is the banquet. His voice is the music. His radiance is the light, and his love is the endless topic of discussion.

JUNE 20

The wise remember the brevity of life. Exercise may buy us a few more heartbeats. Medicine may grant us a few more breaths. But in the end, there is an end. And the best way to face life is to be honest about death.

JULY 13

The price of admission to the Christmas party was a tray of cookies. I can't bake, so I couldn't go. Only moments before the celebration, I was given a gift, a plate of cookies. Did everyone know I didn't bake the cookies I brought to the party? If they didn't, I told them. I told them I was present by virtue of someone else's work. My only contribution was my own confession. We'll be saying the same for eternity.

JUNE 21

I could have gone all day without reminding you of death. We do our best to avoid the topic. One wise man, however, urges us to face it squarely: "We all must die, and everyone living should think about this" (Ecclesiastes 7:2). Solomon isn't promoting a morbid obsession with death. He is reminding us to be honest about the inevitable.

JULY 12

Rest from guilt. Why? Because God leads you in the paths of righteousness.

JUNE 22

"I will fear no evil; for You are with me." Why? Why are these words so treasured? Why is this verse so beloved? We all have to face death. In a life marked by doctor appointments, dentist appointments, and school appointments, there is one appointment that none of us will miss, the appointment with death. "Everyone must die once, and after that be judged by God" (Hebrews 9:27 TEV).

# JULY 11

God hates arrogance. He hates arrogance because we haven't done anything to be arrogant about. Do art critics give awards to the canvas? Is there a Pulitzer for ink? Can you imagine a scalpel growing smug after a successful heart transplant? Of course not. They are only tools, so they get no credit for the accomplishments.

# JUNE 23

Someday our Shepherd will lead us out of the flat lands. He will take us to the mountain by way of the valley. He will guide us to his house through the valley of the shadow of death.

JULY 10

The message of the Twenty-third Psalm is that we have rest, salvation, blessings, and a home in heaven—and we did nothing to earn any of it. Who did? Who did the work? David declares who does. The Shepherd leads his sheep, not for our names' sake, but "for His name's sake."

J U N E   24

You're my place of quiet retreat; I wait for your Word to renew me...therefore I lovingly embrace everything you say.

PSALM 119:114, 119 THE MESSAGE

JULY 9

$W$hy does God have anything to do with us? For his name's sake. No other name on the marquee. No other name up in lights. No other name on the front page. This is all done for God's glory.

JUNE 25

For what the shepherd does with the flock, our Shepherd will do with us. He will lead us to the high country. When the pasture is bare down here, God will lead us up there. He will guide us through the gate, out of the flatlands, and up the path of the mountain.

JULY 8

What you say goes, God, and stays, as permanent as the heavens. Your truth never goes out of fashion; it's as up-to-date as the earth when the sun comes up. Your Word and truth are dependable as ever.

PSALM 119:89-91 THE MESSAGE

# JUNE 26

He knows the path. He has walked this trail many times. Besides, he is prepared. Staff in hand and rod attached to his belt. With his staff he will nudge the flock; with his rod he will protect and lead the flock. He will lead them to the mountains. "Yea, though I walk through the valley of the shadow of death, I will fear no evil; for You are with me; Your rod and Your staff, they comfort me" (Psalm 23:4 NKJV).

JULY 7

God takes the credit, not because he needs it, but because he knows we can't handle it. We aren't content with a bite of adulation; we tend to swallow it all. It messes with our systems. The praise swells our heads and shrinks our brains, and pretty soon we start thinking we had something to do with our survival. Pretty soon we forget we were made out of dirt and rescued from sin.

JUNE 27

Examine me, God...
Make sure I'm fit inside and out
So I never lose sight of your love,
But keep in step with you, never missing a beat.

PSALM 26:2-3 THE MESSAGE

JULY 6

All who make themselves great will be made humble, but all who make themselves humble will be made great.

LUKE 18:14

JUNE 28

Rest from arrogance. Why? Because of his name's sake.

J U L Y  5

Assess yourself honestly. Humility isn't the same as low self-esteem. Being humble doesn't mean you think you have nothing to offer; it means you know exactly what you have to offer and no more. "Don't cherish exaggerated ideas of yourself or your importance, but try to have a sane estimate of your capabilities by the light of the faith that God has given to you" (Romans 12:3 PHILLIPS).

# JUNE 29

Paul said, "The cross of our Lord Jesus Christ is my only reason for bragging" (Galations 6:14). Do you feel a need for affirmation? Does your self-esteem need attention? You don't need to drop names or show off. You need only pause at the base of the cross and be reminded of this: The maker of the stars would rather die for you than live without you. And that is a fact. So if you need to brag, brag about that. And check your chin occasionally.

# JULY 4

Don't take success too seriously. Scripture gives this warning: "When your...silver and gold increase...your heart will become proud" (Deuteronomy 8:13–14). Counteract this pride with reminders of the brevity of life and the frailty of wealth.

# JUNE 30

Demanding respect is like chasing a butterfly. Chase it, and you'll never catch it. Sit still, and it may light on your shoulder. The French philosopher Blaise Pascal asked, "Do you wish people to speak well of you? Then never speak well of yourself." Maybe that's why the Bible says, "Don't praise yourself. Let someone else do it" (Proverbs 27:2).

JULY 3

Celebrate the significance of others. "In humility consider others better than yourselves" (Philippians 2:3 NIV). The truth is, every touchdown in life is a team effort. Applaud your teammates.

J U L Y  1

An elementary-age boy came home from the tryouts for the school play. "Mommy, Mommy," he announced, "I got a part. I've been chosen to sit in the audience and clap and cheer." When you have a chance to clap and cheer, do you take it? If you do, your head is starting to fit your hat size.

JULY 2